WHO IS SHE AND WHAT IS SHE TO YOU?

BY

PRETTY TONY

Published by

World Movement Records

www.worldmovement.com

Copyright © 2010 by Pretty Tony

For information contact
lamont@worldmovement.com
prettytonylv@gmail.com

ISBN: 978-0-982876-80-0

Cover Model: K. Fernandez

www.playasuniversitysygu.com

Printed in the U.S.A

WHO IS SHE AND WHAT IS SHE TO YOU?

As I was writing this it took me back to a time when I was this short fat kid and the confusion I felt, but my saving grace was the older women around me that took me under their wings and schooled me on the ways of women. I have been in their classroom ever since.

But most men never had that, so this is my gift to you, Lexi, that has spent his entire adult life looking for love in strip clubs and in escort services. Diego, who I met at a book signing and he told me that he is in therapy because of loneliness, and how he has to practice stress relief because of severe anxiety when he is in the presence of a woman.

For all the men who have the "I can't get a woman" syndrome or "I don't know how to approach a woman", this is a true playas gift to you because all men do not want to be playas. Thank you for all of the e-mails and letters I hope this helps some of you.

PLAYA STEP YOUR GAME UP

VOL III
ACKNOWLEDGEMENT

I owe a debt of gratitude to so many people and I sometimes forget to mention their names, but nonetheless you mean the world to me.

FROM THE BEGINNING

Ms. Webster, Ms. Mac., Ms. Williams, Ms. Bond - who were the first to push me to live up to my potential.

My Auntie Bev - who has steadfastly stood by me through everything.

Rev. Yvette Noble-Bloomfield - who saw something in me that, at that time, I did not see in myself.

Ms. Keller, Ms. Campbell, Ms. Reece - who helped me time and time again to stay in school.

Mr. Jimmy Lee Gilmer - who taught me patience, and Mrs. Kata Gilmer - for loving me.

Rev. Tom Adams - who helped me to grow as a man.

Mr. Kim Youmans - for putting up with my zany ideas.

Mr. Lamont Patterson, my Partner - thanks for seeing the vision and helping me to make it real.

Mr. Steven Diamond - thank you for everything.

My cousin, Novelette - for always keeping an eye on me.

"Caramia", my other half - thank you for obsessively loving me.

My children, My heartbeats: Cookie, Meara and Soheil, thank you for loving me and saving me.

And most of all, to Miss Williams, my mother - who gave me life, strength and security. Thank you so much. Words cannot truly express my appreciation.

To the following persons - may their souls rest in peace:
My Auntie Icy - thanks for everything.
Mr. Bedasse - thank you for all your kindnesses.
My friend Alrick, Mr. Codner, and last but never least, my cousin Dwight.
Hold up, hold up, hold up, I got some P.I.M.Ps who have also jumped into that cadillac into the sky...
Big Homey Rose - a true pimp and pimp C'r.i.p, also my cousin "Double R" - When we do it, we do it glamorous. So over the top and oh so vegalicious.

I'm Out..

To my beloved "Addie" - you alone knew the reason why you loved me, and you stood in my corner throughout my childhood, you were the rock upon which I built my house and so I'm forever grateful. Time and distance have separated us but you are forever in my heart. A perfect man you may not have been but a man nonetheless who taught me to be strong and never take mess from anyone. Goodbye my "Addie" and know that I am okay...Your Son.

TO MY BROTHERS,

LLOYD, AKA "CURLY"
ANDRE, AKA "SKINNY"
RITCHIE
DAVID, AKA "JAKE THE MULE"
BEVIN
MY DAWG RICHIE RICH
SKIPPY
JAY FISH
K-LOC
SCOOTER
RAII
KELLZ
LLOMZY

TO ALL OF YOU, ONE LOVE .

DOMINUS VOBISCUM

So there I was sitting at my favorite spot on Las Vegas Boulevard, sipping on a mojito and enjoying a rare cool breeze when I saw a vision of beauty walking in a summer dress and it was as though she was perfectly proportioned.

Everything about her seemed to blend together. All I could think was "damn!" I just sat watching her go by and every man that saw her did a double take, and I knew every man was having the same thought. "Can I get some of that?"

That, my dear friends, is called "dick first thinking" and thus the spark for this book was born. I have been in the company of many women in various parts of the world. Some would say that I have had enough for ten men, I have consoled them, I have loved them, spent hundreds of hours talking to them and most importantly listening to them.

On this particular day dozens of conversations with women came pouring into my trend of thought and it was as though all of those encounters were preparing me to put this on these pages and present it to the world. (Names have been changed to protect individuals and not invade their privacy and quite frankly I do not remember most of their names anyway).

Ellissa was an escort, blonde bombshell, 36-24-36 figure, drop dead gorgeous. Her mother was an escort and Ellissa grew up to follow her mother's example with the same pimp. To make her money she had sex with so many different men, women and strange objects that she was numb on the inside, she always told me "I do not give a damn about living."

Beyond the make-up and revealing outfits she was a shell. Her only release was engaging in masochistic sex. She liked being choked until the point of passing out. This was the only way she could get an orgasm.

She was a "speed freak". Crystal meth set her free. Her belief was if she stayed high then she would not remember anything from her past. Men saw her physical beauty and never got beyond her defense mechanism. She was basically ass and tits nothing more. She would self destruct and sabotage any relationship, all the while crying on the inside for love.

So now you are wondering what role I played in her life? I was her confidante, her friend, the only consistent thing she had in her life. This is all I could allow myself to be.

She wanted more but her scars were too deep and she would not let anyone help her heal. Her destructive nature fueled her. One of the silicone implants in her breast ruptured and would cause her severe pain but she would not allow anyone to take her to the doctor.

On numerous occasions I tried to take her to drug rehab and she would literally try to fight me, she would always say things like *"You don't care about me. If you cared about me you would beat me!"*; and *"If it ain't rough it ain't right!"*

Being with her was financially fruitful, so men would be wooed by her generosity and she would shower them with gifts. But as time went by the temper tantrums would become more and more violent.

Their house and car windows would always need repairing; she would constantly try to push a man's button to get a reaction and somewhere in the ensuing chaos, she would find her pleasure.

All the while in her mind this was love, if you offered her kindness in her moments of vulnerability, she would eat it up and almost seem childlike, but the moment would quickly end and she would look at you and say *"you aren't a man you're a punk!"*

Ellissa was a professional agitator. She would disappear for months at a time, then resurface months later emotionally and physically battered and bruised, but just as defiant about taking steps to better herself you almost feel compelled to ask her *"Do you love yourself?"; "If someone really loved you, would they have done this to you?"*

She was a real piece of work. *"What is love?"* She just knew that every man wanted to screw her and there was no exception to the fact. I always wondered what kind of person could get through to her and help her because it would take a lot of patience to get beyond the facade. The frustration was mind blowing dealing with her.

I personally knew two men who truly loved her and

she destroyed both relationships. A lot of you squares get into relationships that you are not prepared to deal with because of misconceptions, never bothering to check into your girlfriends track record.

THINGS ARE NOT ALWAYS
WHAT THEY SEEM, FELLAS.

So let me be one of the first to encourage you to stop thinking with your DICK, see beyond your dick because you might end up with your own ELLISSA as your wife, girlfriend, or baby momma.

"BEAUTY IS ONLY SKIN DEEP"

Have you ever noticed that a woman always has a million questions to ask you, wanting to know where have you been, wanting to know your family, just question on top of question.

PLAYAS UNIVERSITY
Step Your Game Up (S.Y.G.U.)

GENTLEMEN, you have been dazed and misled for a long time, women are just as confused about you as you are about them. Look at all these questions.

Why you always saying you're at the studio but ain't brought one c.d. home..ever?

What do men really want?
What kind of women do men like?
Why won't men open up to a woman?
Why can't men keep their dicks in their pants?
Do all men cheat?
Why wont he grow up?
Why can't he stay out of the streets?
Why does he work so much?
Why can't he stay out of jail?
Why does he feel he has to lie to me for no reason?
Why is he so insecure?
Why wont he stop messing around with his ex-girl?
Why doesn't he listen to me?
Why is he always going over to his baby momma's house?
Why isn't he romantic?
Why is the hood more important than me?
Why does he front on me?
Why are sports more important to him than I am?
Why wont he get a job?
Why does he talk to his mom more than me?
Why wont he marry me?

Why does he tell his baby momma our business?
Why is he so damn possessive?
Why is it that he can ask me questions but I cant do the same?
Why does it seem like we are on two different pages?

Damn, let me stop there because I could write a whole book of questions but anyway the point is this: women are always thinking and scheming, plotting and looking ahead while men are in the moment. You see her. You want her. But what are you getting yourself into? Better yet, how are you going to get her and keep her?

Let me tell you a tale of three little boys sitting on a sidewalk in their neighborhood staring at two beautiful cars. The first little boy said *"When I grow up I want to be a doctor so I can buy a jaguar like that!"*

The second little boy says *"When I grow up I want to be a lawyer so I can buy a Benz like that"*

The third little boy says *"When grow up I want hair all over my body!"*

The other two boys look at him quzzically and say *"Why?"*

The little boy replies *"My sister has a little between her legs and she owns both cars, so I figure if I have hair all over my body I'll be super duper rich!!"* (as told to me by my friend eddie k).

I previously told you about Ellissa and that was the

setup for the lesson, you have been programmed to lust, you have been told to chase. Get that girl.

She has been programmed that all boys want is her S.E.X. Even childhood nursery rhymes knock us, *"Girls are made of sugar and spice and everything nice. Boys are frogs and snails and puppy dog tails"*

Damn, no wonder why many of us have self esteem issues. All you see is the perfumed make up wearing picture she is painting, but there is a lot more going on my friend.

BEFORE YOU PROPOSE MARRIAGE LET ME TELL YOU ABOUT A FEW WOMEN I HAVE MET.

Nalita was a European girl with a thick, rich accent. Very driven to succeed, older men were always her meal ticket and they spoiled her, but none of them ever took the time to school her on how to treat a man. She dished out and they just took it. She was cold and unfeeling. Men were just a means to an end for her. She was a man-eater for sure, but the fault in all of this lies on the shoulders of the sugar daddies who helped create this problem.

Renea was a round-the-way girl: bamboo earrings, lollipops, the whole nine, a straight-up 'apple bottom' wearing, blunt smoking, liquor drinking, round-the-way girl. Brothers always noticed her ass before they acknowledged her and that in itself caused her to have issues. She was an attention freak - needed it all the time.

She could not get enough of it at home, so she kept trying to fill the void, just buck wild, the life of the party. And in that moment that she got plenty of attention, everyone assumed this is all there was to her.

Little did they know that she was really shy and just needed love and wanted to be held and comforted. But the wild personality was what attracted guys. They never stayed around long enough to know her and the list of disappointments just grew.

Sadie was a redhead from the suburbs with a body and boobs that most women pay plastic surgeons for. She could twist herself into some amazing positions and knew how 'to drop it like it's hot'. She was the product of a home with an alcoholic mother, and an abusive stepfather. She would pop any pill she could lay her hands on, and could out drink most men. She specialized in "feeding fools fantasies". She was a force of nature, she would blow into your life and bring a truckload of emotional baggage. Her sex game would leave you with your toes curled and longing for more of her. The magnitude of her issues would eat you up daily, but your dick would not let you walk away.

Jazmine was an older woman who aged gracefully with a banging body [M.L.F]. She had her children very early in life and married out of convenience to ensure that they were well taken care of. She built her whole life around raising her kids, but when they all grew up, she lost her identity and began to look back over her life and found out that her marriage was unfulfilled and had no emotional or physical spark. She started trying to re-capture her youth, hanging out with younger people, throwing parties, and sleeping with her sons friends. Jazmine wanted to be "forever young."

Maria "CHIQUITA BONITA". Her whole identity was built on 'TU QUIERES PAPI.' She considered herself a trophy and men better damn sure work to earn this trophy she stayed in the mirror 24/7. Being in her presence meant constantly reminding her how attractive she was and being reminded how lucky you were that she is in your presence, her sex game was whack, all you could hear was *"don't hurt it!"* or *"you're making it ugly and loose hurry up!"* or *"You can only have it once in awhile!"* But sure enough you simple minded fools lined up because she was eye candy.

Sukee was a rare specimen at 5 feet and 11 inches tall, jet black hair down her back, mixed with white and korean, perfectly sculpted body, with the most amazing smile and warm personality. She just melted your heart. Behind closed doors she was an Asian tigress with powerful sexual prowess, but her flip side was that during sex she would flashback to being molested by her step-brother. Making men salivate was her intent: to bring you to your knees, where she could reclaim the power she lost during her ordeal. She would aim to break you emotionally and financially.

Natasha the nympho or *"Tasha can't say no"*, as I liked to call her, stayed horny morning, noon, and night. Pain made her horny, laughter made her horny, brushing her arm made her horny. She wanted anyone with a dick but some chump was always trying to claim her 'til she slept with his brother, best friend, or sister. She once told me a story about one of her ex-boyfriends that had fallen asleep and his home boy was chilling in the living room playing video games. She purposely walked through the living room naked to go into the kitchen. She got a glass of lemonade, sat down on the couch next to dude and you know the rest. She calmly got up and went into the bedroom with her ex-boyfriend to go to bed and cuddle with him.

Another story went like this: Tasha's best friend broke up with her man and within days Tasha was sexing him. She told me that she did not see a problem with that. She caught one of her boyfriends - I repeat, "one" of her boyfriends - cheating, and flipped out and destroyed his apartment. To this day he probably thinks that it was about him, but she was really mad because she wasn't involved and it could have been a three way hookup.

Destiny was a stripper. She was Creole, outstanding beauty but because of her occupation the very touch of a man made her skin crawl. Men used her as an object of desire. This just mentally destroyed her, but the fast money she made was her addiction. She ended up having a child by a petty insecure square who further destroyed her mind every night. He would ask her the same question, *"who did you sleep with tonight whore?"* She was one of the most graceful women I have ever met, but she was never able to comprehend that she was more than a stripper. Eventually all her issues manifested in the form of obsession with her weight. She eventually started suffering from anorexia.

Stella was this cute, intellectual type from a successful family that ensured that she had all the tools she needed to achieve success. She worked and studied hard, eventually becoming a psychologist, but her weakness was dating and loving 'THUGS'. Time after time they would break her heart because she was a rich girl trying to be bad. They wrecked cars, maxed out credit cards, destroyed her credit, trashed her home, and she still did not have a man. In her mind all men were liars, she was bitter and judgemental, refusing to see that it was her choice in men that led to her heartbreak.

Llorraine was a conservative, hardworking woman. She was a social worker, married for years. She was an everything in its place type, regimented. She built her whole life around her marriage. One day she was at work and wasn't feeling well, so she went home early and found her husband bound and gagged, getting spanked with a paddle by a prostitute, crack pipes and dope on the night stand. Now everything was topsy turvy, nothing made sense. Her structure was gone and uncertainty had taken its place.

Lizzette was this dark chocolate sexy model type. You could picture her wrapping her long legs around you, but she was always dressed in baggy clothing and constantly trying to play the background. Turns out she was molested as a child by her father and brothers, and the only child she had was the product of a rape. She stayed home all the time and had to block the door at night to sleep peacefully. Sudden movements spooked her and she did not trust any man.

Suzanna was a "TOMBOY" who grew up with her brothers and her dad. She was tough and could hang with the boys. She was constantly being mistaken for a lesbian and women were always hitting on her, but she was strictly dickly. She was aggressive and men were sometimes intimidated by this fact. She was always overlooked and this hurt her. Suzanna was genuinely a sweet girl.

Janet had four kids with four different fathers and not one stuck around. They all promised her the world but no one delivered. She always told me that *"my coochie is my curse it's so good that men want it but they never want to stay."* In her entire life she could not think of one good relationship. They started out with a bang but all fizzled in the end and to top it all off she was fighting weight gain. She was hoping one day somebody would stay.

Melanie was the type of girl waiting for "Mr. Right". Saving herself, romance novels, and popcorn were her best friends. She spent so much time alone that her concept of love became warped. She was in love with the idea of being in love, planning a wedding and not even having a groom yet.

Halee was one of the most free spirited persons I ever met. She was not shackled by rules. She lived freely and loved freely. She said what she wanted, and believed that love could be five minutes, five hours, five weeks, five months. Love was free, love was simple, love was a pleasure. Halee loved life, she loved men, she loved freedom. She was seeking her soul mate, someone who felt this way. Men always tried to control her, to curtail her, and she wasn't having that. Her motto was *"If we all get laid, life would be less stressful!"*

Anne Marie, now this girl was special. Raw rage, raw emotion, anger, making men and women submissive was what she was about. She was a "Dominatrix", but running beneath all that was a shy girl, and these two opposing personalities constantly clashed. Whips, chokers, leather belts, the whole nine yards. Something in life triggered her and rage came pouring out.

Eva was an ambitious, focused, young woman. An honor roll student most of her life, she became a successful real estate executive. She was a real "Daddy's girl" spoiled rotten. She compared every man to her daddy, *"My daddy said that if a man can't take care of me better than he can, I don't need a man"; "My daddy said that I'm too much of a woman for any man"; "My daddy said that a man will block my success."* She carried herself with an air of superiority. Eva would try to crush a man's confidence as a test. She was sharp tongued and pulled no punches she would try to slice you up mentally and tell you *"I'm not coming to your pity party!"* Needless to say, her relationships would end with this statement *"I'm not your daddy."*

Lelani was the spiritual type, church every Sunday type, she could quote from genesis to revelations, she was well spoken, well mannered, and well dressed. Lelani was struggling with the fact that she was bi-sexual. Her spirituality and her sexuality were constantly at war. She was raised by strong traditional women, her mom, her aunts, her grand mother. All believed in marriage, children and church, Lelani was buried so far in the closet that she couldn't see daylight.

Tanya was a full figured woman. She spent her whole life competing with smaller women for everything. She did all the things that other girls would not do, but in the end, men always chose looks over heart and loyalty, so she always spent too much time trying to prove herself. Over and over again she was misled, so now she only dates married men, and in her own words *"At least with them I know I'm the other woman!"*

Karen *"I just want a man"* would meet you Monday and by Thursday she was in love. Five minutes after sex, she started planning a wedding. She would pretend to be pregnant, pretend to be sick, put small gashes on her arms to act as though she was committing suicide, lock herself in the bedroom and set fire to trash cans to keep a man. Karen was a drama queen for sure. She would shed crocodile tears at the drop of a dime, leave long voice mails, write ten pages of love letters professing her love, but that would all stop when she found a new love. She took being needy to new heights. I pity her new victims. She was a walking, breathing soap opera. That girl was a real head case.

Alexis was a loving, giving, maturing woman. She just made you want to be a better man. She just made everything feel better. She cooked, cleaned, had a great sense of humor and great looks - the whole package. She had one problem. She was commitment phobic. She was a good friend but she did not want a relationship, and most men found it hard to understand.

Dijonnay was the sassy, sexy and cute kind of woman. Straight up out of "Tha Hood", she was the product of a dysfunctional home - her dad was a thug. He was always locked up and promising her the world but he never kept one promise. Her mom had her early in life and spent her time trying to be forever young. Dijonnay was quick to fight. She did not take mess off anyone. If another woman glanced at her man, an "ass whooping" was in the making. She was possessive and extremely distrustful of other women. She always said *"I don't hang with women. They are scandalous and sneaky"*. She would smother the life out of her relationships.

Cecelia was the artistic type, well traveled and well cultured. She took me to my first opera. She enjoyed each moment of each day and found joy in the simplest things. Her thing was a man had to stimulate her mind. If you could not partake in the beauty that life had to offer, she could not be with you. She was a deep individual, always on a quest to figure out the meaning of life. Most of her relationships got lost in this quest.

Sasha, the seductress, her touch, her kiss, her body, her lips...everything about her would make you want her. She practiced lip positioning in the mirror, she took pride in her sexual skills and she refused to be outdone. Her goal was to devour you completely. She was seeking the man who would stand tall without being over-run by her.

I am telling you about all these women because you must understand that women have issues just like you do.

In my previous novels, I was teaching about mackin and being a playa. This book is about the average guy trying to have a girlfriend or wife. Women are not full of sugar and spice - - don't let your loneliness and low self-esteem cloud your mind.

She is a woman. That's it. She's all full of hormones, estrogen, emotions and moods. She operates differently than you - she is definitely complex, but if you listen and tune in, you might be surprised what you learn.

So here you are, an average guy just looking for love or just to get laid, kicking back admiring women, hoping and wishing one will notice you, but they all passed you as usual.

First of all, stop placing women on a pedestal. You are setting yourself up for disappointment. Whether you are tall, fat, skinny, shy or stupid, there are women who date your type. Please believe that. The difference between men and women is that women know their type. They know what kind of men they attract and what kind of men they are attracted to - that is why they say things like " *You are really not my type*"; *'I only date ballers' '*; "*I only date tall men*"; "*I only date thugs*"; "*I only date older men*"; "*I only date a specific zodiac sign*" etc., etc., etc.

Be it right or wrong they know their type. While on the other hand men are just lustful, we're all impulse, action and machismo. If a woman approaches us we don't care about knowing if she is our type - we just want to hit it. Do you know what type of women you attract? Take a minute and think about that.

Is your answer *"whoever will let me hit it"*? Then you will have a lot to learn. Average Joe, this is something you need to figure out. Anyway, there are some basic principles and steps that will further your success in dealing with women.

Average Joe, you need to start packaging yourself. Think of yourself as new product being placed on the market. How you are going to stand out in the crowded market-place? Look in the mirror and visualize a conversation with a woman. Practice your introduction, and don't stutter. Do not act overwhelmed, act like you belong in that moment. Better yet, know that you belong in that moment - nothing too rehearsed, just flow. Don't pretend to be anything but what you are. Pretending only works for hook-ups. Over time, your true colors will show.

Don't be afraid of rejection. Not every woman will like you - in the game it's hit or miss. Let me tell you about my homey. We called him 'Midnight' - turn the lights off and all you saw were teeth. (Ha ha waddup dawg, I'll holla at you soon).

Anyway, he was butt ugly. But my homey had two things that separated him from other ugly cats - he was always 'fresh' from head to toe, and he could dance circles around everybody. When he was on the dance floor he owned it, and the women just loved that. They would be on him like white on rice. The point being that Midnight did not dwell on his weakness, he focused on his strengths and made sure everyone else focused on them too. So that is what made him appealing. So "STEP YOUR FRESH UP".

So what are you good at? Are you a good cook? Women love a man who can cook. Are you an avid reader? Join book clubs, so that you can show off your literary prowess. Are you a sensitive poet? Go to poetry readings and pour your heart out. The women there will feel your pain. Are you a big dude? B.B.W. CLUBS ARE ALL OVER THE INTERNET. (In case you don't know, big beautiful women). Also, certain cultures from other countries hold big men in high regards. If you're a nerd find somewhere that showcases your intellect. The women there will dig you.

Surround yourself with an environment that lets you get your shine on. If you're on internet porn sites, calling sex lines, and spending your nights home with your insecurities as your best friend, then KY JELLY and VASELINE will be your only companionship, along with Ms. Palm-er and her five daughters.

You are slacking and lacking on gaining valuable social experiences. There are too many women desperately seeking, but how are you going to find then if they are not aware of you. If you are unable to communicate with women, the disconnect you feel will become worse.

NEWSFLASH

As confused as you are about women, they feel the same about men. They are just better at masking their confusion. I'm going to present some questions that support my claim and show you the facts:

Why do men never stop to ask questions?
Why do men judge women by the way they dress and the way they walk?
Why do men use stupid pick up lines?
Why do men think they are God's gift to women?
Why do men think foreplay is not important?
Why do men always try to prove their manhood?
Why do men think with their dicks?
Why do men wait for days before calling a woman?
Why do men act tough but have soft egos?
Why don't men listen to their women?
Why do men always grab their dicks?
Why don't men show their true feelings?
Why don't men think before they open their mouth?
Why do men ask questions that they really don't want the answers to?
Why do men say things behind closed doors but then flip the script in public?
Why can't men just hang out with women without scheming on having sex?
Why do men lie about the size of their dicks?
Why do men always try to dominate the conversation?
(QUESTIONS REQUIRE ANSWERS AND IF THEY HAD THE ANSWERS THEY WOULD NOT ASK QUESTIONS).

Now then, you have seen men who women naturally gravitate towards and this has puzzled you. Don't let this block your progress. Work on developing your own swagger. Here are some basics. You need "The Four P's": packaging, pursuit, pockets, personality.

Personality is extremely important, as this makes a woman take notice of you. Continually work on your verbal skills, because no one is interested in a person that is as exciting as a brick wall. Work on having a sense of humor, laughter always eases the mood. Find out about her and find common areas of interest. DO NOT BROWN NOSE! Allow her to get into you, pick your spot in the conversation and make the conversation flow.

Be a gentleman, open doors, pull chairs out. Chivalry is an old school element that never fails. Now this is very important, DO NOT GO TO PLACES YOU CANNOT AFFORD! Keep it real. If Denny's is what you can afford do not go to Red Lobster. Stay within your budget.

Here is the lowdown if the date is a success: she is getting to know the real you. If the date is a bust, you won't be broke, busted, and disgusted. If she is into you, she will want to see you again and by all means you should let her know that her company was something you really enjoyed, and that you will really like to see her again.

Now comes **Packaging**. Have you ever seen a playboy looking like he got dressed out of a thrift store? HELL NO! Get your wardrobe together, stop wearing your old flannel shirt. Get a few nice outfits to wear out on the town. Do not try to be too flamboyant. Gators, snake skin and ostrich shoes are not for everyone. In other words, let everyone respect your fresh. Keep your fingernails clean because women take notice of them, your shoes are very important, they should be maintained and un-scuffed. Keep breath mints on you and try to project a calm and confident demeanor. Do not be too cocky and grabby - this is a for sure turn-off. And let me reiterate - wear clothes that compliment you.

No matter your size, shape or height, make sure you are working your mojo. When you look good, you feel good. You feel it in your walk, you feel it in your swagger.

That leads me straight into the next point: **Pursuit.** This is what separates the men from the boys. You have to pursue a woman. Entice her. This is part of the eternal quest for manhood, but know this: not every woman you pursue will be interested - make your advance and wait for her response. If she is not into it, keep it moving and learn from your interaction, the knowledge is priceless.

View it all as a learning experience. Do not take things personally. Practice makes you better conditioned mentally and emotionally, so as you sharpen your skills you will find that you stumble and bumble much less - applying yourself to these disciplines will eventually bear fruit.

Getting the things we want in life is never easy, show this woman that you think she is worth the time and effort. Separate yourself from the next "man". Now, in saying this I do not mean "obsessing or stalking" - e.g. calling her 15 times per day (that is stalking). If she has not returned your call - let it go. E-mailing her everyday, you are coming off as very desperate (this is only acceptable if both parties are mutually e-mailing). KNOW WHEN IT IS TIME TO BACK-OFF.

Pockets. Without some kind of income you cannot shine, and the other elements will not work. You've got to treat yourself and then you can treat others IT COSTS TO BE THE BOSS. You have to put the pieces together - be consistent in your efforts to make yourself more appealing.

WHAT IS SHE TO YOU?

Now let's assume that you are dating this girl you have been pursuing. There are things you need to know about the woman you're dating. When you date her you're dating:

A	Her ex-boyfriends
B	Previous hurts
C	Her life history
D	Her expectations
E	Her childhood insecurities
F	Her friends who do or do not like you
G	Her parents
H	Her kids (if she has kids)
I	Her imagination
J	Her disappointments
K	Her monthly cycle
L	Her fantasies

Make sure you are mentally ready to deal with these things because they all surface over time. Are you man enough to deal? Once the euphoria of getting this girl wears off reality sets in, and now here she is - what's next? Is this someone you can see yourself being around for awhile? Is she worth the effort?

Sometimes we men tend to hang our hats too high and get women who are truly out of our league. You go so far out of your way! GET IN WHERE YOU FIT IN!!! Be real, dawg, look at yourself and decide - could I truly mentally handle having a dime piece in my life knowing that everywhere you go other men will be on her - are you ready for that? If she is a showstopper and you are not, it will magnify your shortcomings. APPLY SOME DAMN COMMON SENSE DAWG! Now here are your guidelines:

Check her track record
What is she about?
Is she wife/girlfriend material?
(You can't make a ho a housewife)
Does she have baby daddy drama?
What is she looking for?
Is she on the same page as you?
Beyond physical attraction, what else do you see in her?
Does she share areas of common interest?
Does she want to participate in your life? or
Does she want you to change your whole life to accommodate her?
Does she satisfy you?
Can she satisfy you?
Ask questions about what she expects of you?

Does she take interest in your passions?
Is she someone you want to have kids with?
If you are a missionary type of guy and she is a freak. what are you going to do?
What baggage is she dragging around with her?
Most importantly, What are you looking for?
Can she provide it?

You, sir, are the captain of your ship so act like it. Ask questions dawg, but if your ego is soft, let bygones be bygones. Example: there was a guy who had a hot girlfriend and their life was cool. One day she told him that she had made an amateur porn tape five years prior to meeting him, and he was fascinated by this, he begged over and over again to see the tape and she would turn him down time after time. She finally gave in and one day they watched together. She was in the film with two guys and they were turning her out, and she was loving it. At first he tried to play cool and act as if it didn't affect him but it slowly ate him up and he could not perform his manly duties with her anymore because he thought he was not man enough. This guy ruined a great relationship by being a dumb ass. He should have left her video in the past. Gentlemen, you have to grow up and realize that no one is perfect.

Do you enjoy her company?
What role do you want her to play in your life?
What role does she want to play in your life?
Do the two roles coincide?
Can you stand the sound of her voice?
(Remember this is the voice you will hear for awhile).

Can this woman positively affect your life?

There are many men on this planet that regret the day they ever laid their eyes on their exes because on their arrival into the man's life misery became his best friend. Then there are men who met women who brought sanity to their lives. She brought focus, she brought love.

Gentlemen, decision-making is the key element. This is the secret of your future love life: DECISION-MAKING SKILLS - GREAT SEX DOES NOT MEAN LOVE. Beautiful face does not mean beautiful person, flattering tongue does not mean truth. Convenience is not commitment - be wise, be realistic. Stand up for yourself and see if she will stand up for you.

So I have told you these things, I hope someone is listening. Remember, if you are a good man you deserve a good woman...You must always remember where she ends and you begin.

Do not be absorbed by a relationship/friendship that you neglect your first priority - YOU. KEEP YOUR "STAR PLAYER" IN FOCUS.

LIFE

As I ride on this train called "Life", there are many junctions and crossroads. At some of the stops, I pick up new baggage and as the ride gets longer some of the baggage proves to be too heavy so I must set them aside

- sometimes even swallow my pride because some of the baggage become badges that I wore to say:

This is why! This is how! This is when! And I am because of this!

But truth be told I'm better off without some of the baggage that was wearing me down, for now I rarely frown, and even greater is the fact that I'm no longer a clown.

So the train slows down and I see her at the station. Her face shows her frustration, so I speak and share my elation, I extend an invitation for her to share this ride with me. I tell her to leave some of her baggage behind, so that we don't go over the weight limit, so we check how much baggage we have, and shed some irrelevant items. The train rolls out of the station, we form a union, a friendship, a bond, and our journey begins. Day turns to night, night turns to day, days to weeks, weeks to months, months to years, and throughout our journey we shed many fears, and only a few tears, on this journey of life.

GOTTA HAVE THAT

The thrill is the hunt
The moment when you see her
Your eyes are glued to her body frame
Just physical attraction
Pure magnetism
Your every thought says "touch that!"
Make her moan
Nothing else matters
Common sense, consequence
Nothing matters
"Get that, Get that!"

Words can't express this raging lust
Night nurse, quench my thirst
You are my medication
For this burning desire
So across the room I go to this honey I need to know.

A HOOD STORY

I grew up on this street called sorrow, two blocks over
from Broken Dream Boulevard
My best friend's name was My Gat
My first girlfriend was called Hoodrat
The school I went was Hustlas Academy
Then I moved to University of Hard Knocks
Cum Laude.
I had an uncle called "Sam" who made a lot of promises,

but never gave a damn, and never kept one.
My father name was Mr. Never Around and my block
was my proving ground.

So what do you expect from me, "huh?"
My mother's name was Ms. Doing the Best She Can
Mr. Lock Your Ass Up was the local cop
I had a couple of homeys called
Down for Whatever
Get this Money
Just Don't Give a Damn
and Cap that Fool

Dream turn to nightmares, quickly in my head, so maybe
I don't dream but I damn sure scheme.
What's that you say?
Who would I like to meet?
The only person I would like to meet is Mr. Please Can I
Get Outta Here
Opportunity has not knocked on my door for awhile, and
Mr. Trust got shot down the block.
Miss Love is cool but she is straight-up misunderstood
because she is so hard to define.
Joey Crime - that fool is always in my hood and his
partner Drama is always right behind that fool.
Together they got my hood on lock, I want to get on the
path of possibilities, but the road of realities all blocked
by Gang Bangin' Gary.
So there it is another day in my hood.

So this is our starting point - this is where we're from and understanding this will reveal our attitudes and mind- sets.

Gentlemen, we must embrace change - don't let the hood define us. So many of us want to try new things, but fear and ignorance hold us back.

Let me be one of the first to tell my "Street Soldiers" that there is a whole world of possibilities out there, but we will have to polish ourselves up. It is ok to want more, it is okay to be better than your circumstances, so here I am telling you to open up your mind and let a real mother......... spit at you.

The hood has taken so much from us and given very little in return. Fast money is a come up, not a career. Use it for a start and leave it behind - it is part of the ball and chain that keep us trapped to the streets.

Most of us, before we turn eighteen have lost friends to death and long term lock down that hardens us to no longer believe we can escape - trust me, we can get out.

Sometimes even when negativity is all we know, we must keep dreaming, keep believing, keep pushing and things will turn around. Do not let the circumstances of life in the hood define you - our life, my life, your life - is worth something.

QUINTESSENTIAL RULES OF BEING A MAN
(some rules have been previously stated)

A   Never be afraid to express yourself

B   Your emotions should not be worn on your shirt sleeves. Embrace them and learn to address them

C   Do not be clingy and constantly paranoid. What is to be will be in a relationship!

D   Do not set yourself up for failure by undermining the trust and sanctity of your relationship.

E   LEAD! Do not follow, it is your inherent right, but respect your significant other's opinon, value their contributions and what they have to offer.

F   Know what you are and make sure you are comfortable with yourself, because no material possession or another person can validate you.

G   Your mother is to be respected but her interference in your personal life should be minimal.

H   Your homeys are your boys but keep them out of your bedroom affairs because there is always one secretly wanting your woman.

I   A grown man always has a plan and a back-up plan

J   Do not get caught up in a he said, she said, they said!

K   A woman cannot tell a man how to be a man

L   Learn from your mistakes.

M   Do not live your life in the rear view mirror.

N   Don't let your jealousy override your good sense

O   A genuine level of maturity is a must to be a man.

P   Carry no issues from your last relationship into the new.

Q   Treat your woman the same in public as in private.

R   It is okay to talk to your lady and tell her how

you feel.

S   Condoms save lives, use them. HIV and AIDS are everywhere.

T   Even though she thick, that is not proof that she is clean, this is nonsense.

U   Even though our fathers were shady we can be better men than they could ever be.

V   A tattoo on a broad means nothing.

W   Never let a situation push you to the point of violence because while you are locked down she will be doing whatever she wants to anyway. Then who is really looking stupid? You ain't no punk - if you walk away, you are smart.

X   The sweetest revenge is success, not falling for the trap of *"you ain't never going to be shit"* Shine, shine, shine.

Y   No "bitch-assness" you're not a woman - so don't act like one (this is true of some men that were raised by their sister and mom. Trust me, you pick up some of their traits and you don't even know it)

15 THINGS NOT TO DO

1.   Do not constantly compare her to your ex-girlfriend.

2.   Do not constantly probe about her ex-boyfriend (this is extremely annoying)

3.   Do not say stupid things like:

4.   "Did he do you like this?

5.   "Was his penis bigger than mine!?

6.   "See how good I am to your kids!"

7. "Am I a better lover!?
8. "Did you do the things to him like you do to me?"
9. "How come you can't move like she could?"
10. He can't see his kids I am their daddy now!"
    (Now if the dude isn't taking care of his
    responsibility then all bets are off).
11. Do not put a cape on and try to save a woman if
    she is not trying to save herself
12. Stop hearing footsteps in the dark, they may well
    be your imagination. Be observant and informed.
13. Do not take a small issue and make a major
    confrontation of it.
14. Do not allow your old habits to disrupt your new
    ways.
15. Do not accept the input of homeys who are still
    living the way you were ten years ago.

Your life is not a music video
Your life is not a movie
Your life is not a song

Every man is not cut out to be a playa and every
man is not cut out to be a pimp, be an individual and make
your life work for you. Think before you act, develop your
own philosophy.

We have this thing about 'keeping it real' - let me
tell you what is real. If you have a woman/wife/baby
momma that is good to you - cooks, cleans and does right
by you - show her some respect. You are not soft if you tell
her you love her. You are not weak if you go home rather
than KICK IT. Everything in life has its place and nobody

has taught us that.

If we get locked up we write letters to our girls telling her to stay down with us and telling her to love us, together forever. Why not do it while we're free? You expect her to come see about you when things are bad, so be good to her when things are rolling. How many homeys write to you when you on lock? Which one is going to your crib, trying to holla at your broad? Loyalty has to be called into question when you talk about the hood. The "G" Code has to be rewritten and respected.

Hoodrats are community property to be shared - stop trippin over a hoodrats wifey is off limits (only one woman at a time can be tagged wifey) so choose wifey carefully. Now, as a man, if you live in a household of your own. Weed, alcohol and new kicks take a back seat, to your rent and your utilities (light, gas, etc). Carry your weight homey.

THE CURSE

A lot of you brothers end up with kids by the neighborhood "jump off", aka "Drop the Drawse Delilah" and the drama begins with you arguing and trippin' because there is always somebody kickin it at her house. Did you really think she would change? She is living the life she has chosen and your dick is just another dick in the long lives of the dicks she has chosen. You coming by and calling collect when you are on lock doesn't mean nothing - you catching a case for domestic violence is STUPID!

Or being charged with "terrorist threats" - come on, dawg, she was, is, and will always be a hoodrat! It is her life.

The question now becomes how do you deal with the games she plays?

(A)   If you care about the child/children, man the hell up! Anger, violence, arguing and drama are not beneficial.

(B)   Establish a paper trail that shows your participation in the kid/kids' life.

(C)   Instead of new rims, kicks and liquor, hire an attorney to fight for your rights.

(D)   If you hustle, start a home business on paper to show income.

(E)   Walk away from the set-up of arguing with latest brother in her life.

(F)   Wear a damn condom and you won't have to do any of this!!

"Jump offs" are there for temporary enjoyment and practice.

"Gold Diggers" - they only have one intention to get what they can, and some of you fools literally break yourselves, give and give and she takes and takes.

" If you want me then buy this for me!"

"I need some new shoes to match the outfit you bought!"
"Can you pay all my bill for me?!

She has an attitude when you can't buy her something and belittles you in the process. Sometimes she even takes your money and give it to another man and your dumb ass just keeps on giving.

Now, if your attraction is sexual and that is being taken care of, that's cool! But if you are in love and planning a future then the words "chump", "trick" and "fool" come to mind. The sad part is that "Gold Diggers" are not hard to spot, they do not hide who they are - trust me.

PLAYOLOGY UNIVERSITY

Motto

This is the place for men to come and gain insight and understanding about themselves, and how to improve their swagger, how to step into manhood, and a wide variety of topics that deal with us.

TODAY I SAW LIFE MANIFEST

A child entered into this realm today
She is from somewhere else
But somehow she found me
I am not sure what to make of her yet
She is not sure what to make of me as yet

So we are locked in this eternal dance of love
She may save me yet time will tell
Time will tell

HAVE I SOLD MY SOUL FOR THIS COOCHIE?

What lengths do men go to for some sexual satisfaction?
Ruined lifelong relationships
Turned their backs on family
Financial ruins, losing control of all they hold dear
All for this mesmerizing, puzzling, questionable woman.
All that matters is her touch, her presence, her vaginal
essence. The very thought of her makes you tingle,
Wherever you are there the thought of her holds your
mind.
The thought of someone else touching her just unleashes
uncontrollable rage. The way she moans and says you're
the one, just makes you feel like a man.

She tells you no one has ever been this deep in her before,
She tells you no one has made her feel this way before,
You are the man who can make her feel like this - only me...
What part of me is truly left?
Where does she end and begin? It is as though I am
addicted to this coochie.

Gentlemen, this is a genuine story be careful what you
wish for and want in your life.

THE NOW OF MY LIFE

If all I have is this moment, then why would I waste it on misery. I have an expiration date and this is certain. My life, my memories, my thoughts, my feelings, my very aura are only here for this moment - so if I give it to misery and negativity what is left for me?

I sit and often wonder just what is it that my moment will amount to. It feels as though some measure of darkness is constantly in pursuit of me, could this really be true? It manifests itself in the form of friends, family, strangers, but here is something I have learned: Step back and become hater/negativity proof, let those who seek to bring you down drift away from you no matter who they are - live your life to the fullest my friend.

LIFE IN THE REARVIEW MIRROR

Have you ever stopped and thought about some things you have done in the past? And you just shake your head because they seem so stupid, and at the time you thought you were doing the right thing. As each day goes by we should learn something more but life has a way of distracting you. So at some point we must learn from the mistakes of the past. We can't change yesterday. Today is all we have and I know that we sometimes would like a do-over but what is done is done. You can atone for some actions and events but leave most things behind. As youngsters, we said and did immature things but I implore you to live your life to the fullest, because this life is temporary and all we have is this moment. We all have an expiration date, so the question is what are you doing with???? As today fades away I am sharing my moment with you.

MY PHILOSOPHY

Stand for something.
Know who the hell I am.
Learn to choose my battles.
Know when to go hard and when to fall back.
Accept people for who they are and not what I want them to be.
My destiny is my own to pursue and obstacles are there to be overcome.
Bend but never break.
Understand that my trials and tribulations are molding me into a man.
From the ashes of the past, a better man will emerge.
I am not God's gift to women but I am damn sure a gift to the world.
I'm the king of my domain and anyone I permit to enter my domain will respect my world.
Sex is not an occupation it is a hobby (a pleasurable hobby).
I will not permit a coward's heart to beat in my chest.
I shall express how I feel at all times so that I am not misunderstood.
My thoughts are my own.
I will not permit someone else's negativity to be my downfall.
I validate myself and only the universe that create me, qualifies to judge me.

NOT KNOWING WHAT I AM FEELING

Because we're men we're taught that only girls cry or you have to be tough. So we go through unable to express our emotions or just how we feel. The only emotion that we can readily express is anger and we become good at that because it fuels our machismo. I'm not saying wear your feelings on your sleeves but there comes a moment when a man must be able to freely say what he feels without being conflicted on the inside because he feels soft or weak.

Gentlemen, we're human beings not animals and the universe provided us with the ability to think and express thoughts, so learn to process what is in your heart, what is in your soul, what is it that brought you to this moment. Tragedy should not be the only time you openly show feelings. Say what you mean, one word at a time.

SO MUCH MORE TO LIFE THAN SEX

Ultimately the time, energy and effort spent in pursuit of momentary satisfaction must not be more than the time you spend in understanding yourself and the various aspects of your life.

THINK BEYOND THE TIP
OF YOUR DICK, GENTLEMEN

Even though a young lady may be attractive on

the surface, what is hidden deep beyond those delicious breasts is what you should be asking yourself.

PLACING TOO MUCH VALUE ON GOOD SEX

Too many of us as brothers place a high premium on sex. We spend an extraordinary amount of time, effort and money in the pursuit of a fleeting moment.

We lose our very soul and at times, placing all else on the sidelines, business, friendships, family and, of course, our good senses.

Gentlemen, everything has a time and a place, trust me when I tell you this. Think of your life as though it is a pie chart. Give each thing in your life a slice of the pie and divide it up. We must have priorities, needs and wants. We must know the difference between each one

MONEY AND THE MAN

So another day and things feel the same. More bills, less money and those at the top trying to squeeze blood from a turnip. A brother standing and looking at the course of his life, and frustration just grows. But I look into my kids' eyes and I see eternal hope. My daughter says her first words, *"come here daddy"*. My boy is healthy and strong. These small blessings give me the strength to keep on fighting. So money is vital but it does not define my life.

WHAT THE HELL IS A MAN TO DO?

At the end of the day, all that I can do is to be the best that I can be, sometimes in a relationship that may not be good enough, but I refuse to be what somebody else wants me to be. This is the fire in my soul, it took me a long time to grow into this skin, so accept me for what I am because no one is perfect. I walk this, I talk this, I live this - this is my life.

MAKING THE MOST OF WHAT I GOT

So you're limited with what life has given you. You're not handsome, you're not rich. You're not blessed with a six pack. You're not tall and sexy. Does this mean you're not capable of being attractive to women?

Gentlemen, when you're given lemons you make lemonade or if you prefer lemon water, make the best of what you have to work with. Beating yourself up will only make your life worse. If you need help, spend time with me. There is so much to learn. We make things happen and life is always throwing twists and turns at us. Adjust, adapt and keep it moving.

HERE I STAND

So now I have met her and we're getting to know each other. How do I proceed? Many times that is how a man feels. We're caught between sexual desire and actual emotions. Is she a one hit and quit or is she wifey material?

Gentlemen, the answer to that question can only be provided by time - yes, time. Because if she give up the drawse quickly, that can mean various things.

First you think she is easy but it could also mean she really vibed off you. So you need time to see what she is all about. It could mean she was really lonely and needed male companionship. But once again, only time to check her story will validate that.

Then again maybe this is a regular activity and only time around will let you know if she a "Diana Drop the Drawse" type. So I suggest hold up on the floodgate of emotions and give it the time it needs to operate.

CUPID'S CURSE / CUPID'S BLESSINGS

Ironic isn't it that the very emotion that can bring calm to trouble life is the same emotion that can fuel jealousy and hatred. How is this possible? Is this some kind of joke the universe has played upon us?

Cupid comes in and just changes everything. What was important before Cupid arrived is no longer important. How can I be me when cupid is running the show? But at the same time so much has gotten better. But this is unchartered waters, there are no guidebooks and my mistakes are magnified. So trial and error is my only way So many men feel like this. Well, this is the place to work through all this.

The experience I have gained, I am willing to share. The first step is the book "PLAYOLOGY'. This brings you into the realm then we can work from there

PLAYAOLOGY UNIVERSITY

TOO MANY men have the "Grass is Greener" Syndrome. Why are men so envious of another man's wife/ girlfriend?

This is so common all around us, a stranger, a friend, a family member. They sit and stew and plot. They say things like *"why can't I have a girl like that"*

Hater get your mind right. Women are plentiful but you CHOOSE to focus your desire on another man's main squeeze. They say things like *"he can't handle that"* but they can't hide - watch the eyes, the eyes are the window of the soul.

They sit and play tattletale behind your back and she eats it up not realizing that there are ulterior motives. And even if she knows of his hidden agenda she plays her role, be it vulnerable, be it flirtatious, be it damsel in distress.

And his male ego kicks in and he feels that he is closer to the smell of her underwear. Gentlemen, this is life unfolding before you. Do not let your ego pump you up to believe that you can treat a woman like crap that leaves room for the haters to creep in. Even if you are good to her, the haters are still lurking. Jealousy is their everyday occupation

DEFINING A PLAYA

The environment I am from was hard. You had to have skills to survive. A Playa is someone who learned to navigate the hood and knew all the right moves, spoke with the latest slang, they made talking to women seem easy, they wore the latest fashions, they carried themselves with just seamless swagger. This was the person who was always in the mix

THE PLAYA MOTTO

'To have something you have to be about something"
Stay focused and stay grinding.

THIS IS THE JOURNAL OF A REAL PLAYA

The books I have written are available worldwide. I am the Chairman of the Worldwide Playa Association and Professor emeritus of PLAYAS UNIVERSITY S.Y.G.U.

We as men tend to underestimate women, but at the same time overvalue them, we as men are not defined by a woman, stand tall and take hold of yourself.

So few of us have good role models to provide us

with the guidelines we need to understand our place in this life, but I have lived and learned and I am willing to share my life experience.

So the first question is where do I stand in my life? How do I go about getting my grown man on? How do I present myself to the world?

LOUIE
(Dedicated to all those who never had a chance at life)

Expectation unrealized
Potential untapped
Destiny unfulfilled
My dear friend, life has taken any chance of normalcy
from you, and you have fallen to the wayside.
What a cruel twist of fate, so I proudly write these
words to let the world know of your existence and no
matter your circumstance, know that I your brother have
never forgotten you.
So may the universe wrap its ever loving arms around
you and may your life be blessed.
And I hope the angels will watch over you.
May patience be granted to those that care for you,
to all those that we've lost, words cannot express the
emptiness.
We shall live on for you.